PORTRAIT OF STEAM

Eric Treacy — Footplate Bishop

Portrait of Steam

Eric Treacy

PRC

This edition published in 1991 by
The Promotional Reprint Company Limited
for Bookmart Limited (Registered No. 2372865)
Desford Road, Enderby, Leicester, U.K.

ISBN 1 85648 010 0

First published in 1967 by Ian Allan Ltd
Reprinted 1993

©Millbrook House Ltd

Printed and bound in China

INTRODUCTION

I MUST say, I never thought "Lure of Steam" would go as well as it did.

Naturally, I was delighted when I received a large number of appreciative letters from those who did not think that 63/- was too much to pay for a collection of my railway photographs.

I brought a very critical eye to the book. There were a number of pictures that I wanted to replace, if, and when, the book ran to a second printing. My suggestion to this end was received by Ian Allan with the proposal that if I still had material that I wanted to use, I should launch into another book. Although I thought that I really had shot my bolt photographically with "Lure of Steam", I could not resist this invitation to do an "encore".

And "Portrait of Steam" is the result. I think this really is the end of my publishing exercises, for I have about exhausted my stock of negatives.

A convenient attack of pneumonia and its consequent period of convalescence have enabled me to do much of the preparation of this book.

I think that I can anticipate some of the criticisms that will follow its appearance.

Some will say that there is too much in it: too much repetition. A criticism with which I shall agree. My answer is that this is a "Portrait", and, as such, is an attempt to show the steam engine in every kind of setting and mood, and in pictures which have given me much pleasure in the taking.

It is an impression, rather than a well balanced selection.

There will be some who will comment that pictures are included which are already familiar to those who have been regular readers of the various railway journals.

Yes, I accept that, but I answer it by saying that a number of people have asked that I include some of my better known pictures in this final book from my camera.

Nearly twenty years ago, I published a book called "Steam Up", long since out of print. I have repeated in this book one or two illustrations from that book because I have been asked to.

However, it is not for me to defend myself! I was asked to do this book by the publisher, and I have done it. If he thinks that it will attract sufficient customers to justify its publication—good for him! And for me!

And so, greetings to all who have loved the steam engine: to those who have designed, built, maintained, cleaned, fired, and driven the steam engine.

May this book, for you, keep the memory fresh, and be for your children, and your children's children, a glimpse of a world they never knew: a world which, whatever its strains and stresses, produced that great kettle on wheels, with its coal scuttle behind—the STEAM LOCOMOTIVE.

Eric Treacy

CONTENTS

THE ROAD TO CARLISLE
Portrait of a Journey

THE first time I rode on the footplate of an engine was sometime in the 1930's. The engine was one of Fowler's Royal Scots, and the train was the 8.15 a.m. Liverpool to Euston.

I rode as far as Crewe. The driver was Walter Freestone of Camden Shed.

The last time I rode on the footplate was two or three years ago. The engine was a Britannia Pacific, and the train was the down Thames-Clyde Express. I rode from Leeds to Carlisle. The driver was Tommy Gibbs of Holbeck Shed.

Between the first and last trips, there were many other footplate journeys. On A3 Pacifics with the North Briton from Leeds to Newcastle; on A4 Pacifics from Leeds to King's Cross; on re-built Scots from Leeds to Carlisle; on Duchess Pacifics from Carlisle to Euston and return; on Jubilee's, Black 5's, and Baby Scots.

They have all been exciting journeys; at least, exciting to me, if not to the crew. Always I have been welcome on the footplate. Often, I have taken my turn with the shovel, and sometimes, under very watchful supervision, I have handled the regulator.

Some routes are more to be remembered than others, as are some engines.

I think that my favourite route is from Leeds to Carlisle, via Settle. It has something of everything.

First, there is the unashamed industrialism of Leeds. Factories, mills, steel works, gas works, power stations, countless chimneys staining the sky with their filth: but there is a grandeur about this, because there is no pretence about it.

Soon this gives way to smaller towns like Keighley, Bingley, and Skipton. Towns, as I know well, with a rugged individuality of their own, in which people work hard and play hard. For all that, they are towns with thriving industries, which have not conquered the moors and hills in which they are set. The line is edged with small-holdings: sheep that are blacker than nature meant them to be, graze on the hill sides, and glare indignantly at passing trains.

In the Craven country, north of Skipton, the air is cleaner, ahead there are signs of the hill country through which the railway finds its way. In the summer there is the smell of the newly cut grass; away to the west there is the long flat back of Pendle Hill, and to the east, the hills above Wharfedale. Gargrave and Bell Busk are soon past, as the train draws into Hellifield, which is a typical railway town. An ugly station with a long island platform, and a lot of little houses built towards the end of the last century for the railway community. Hellifield's importance arises from the fact that it is a junction at which the old Midland line to Scotland is joined by the line from Lancashire: traffic from Manchester, Burnley and Blackburn finds its way north via Hellifield.

So far, the journey has been easy—the Long Drag is about to begin. For a few miles out of Hellifield the gradient is slightly with the engine, then, shortly after, the line to Carnforth and Morecambe takes itself off to the left at Settle Junction, the hard work begins.

The cut off is lengthened and there's a good deal more noise up front, as we climb up the valley of the Ribble. There are thirteen miles at 1 in 100 ahead.

As we cross the viaduct at the north end of Settle, we catch a glimpse of this attractive Yorkshire market town, then we are at it. The country has changed—there are still green fields, but all round us are the limestone outcrops. This is the country of the pot-holes; underground caves with intriguing names like Alum Pot and Gaping Ghyll.

If it isn't raining, as it nearly always is in these parts—to the east of Horton in Ribblesdale, you will see Pen-y-Ghent. Not a very high mountain, but it looks big because it rises straight out of the valley: in shape, not unlike a large animal on its haunches.

By now, the engine is beginning to gasp a bit, and the fireman is too, especially if there is a fierce cross wind from the west finding its way between the coaches and acting as a brake.

Ribblesdale is, perhaps, the least frequented of the Yorkshire dales. It is a wild, savage place with none of the lush prettiness of Wharfedale. There are some, amongst whom I count myself, who give Ribblesdale pride of place amongst the Yorkshire dales—just because it is wild and savage.

And how right a belching steam engine is in this setting.

The valley is widening now: everywhere there are sheep: here and there a lonely farmstead nestles behind a clump of trees. Up here the sky is always magnificent—there is always plenty of it, and the cloud formations are the painter's joy.

To the west, there comes into view the black mass of Ingleborough, not Yorkshire's highest hill. But it looks as if it were. It has a curious flat top, on which, tradition has it, horse races were once held.

Through Ribblehead station, out on to the Batty Moss Viaduct. Straight up the valley from the west blow the westerly gales, and many a tarpaulin cover has been whipped by the wind off the trucks of goods trains as they cross this magnificent viaduct. Very welcome to the local farmers are these tarpaulins—so I am told.

The train is slowing now as it approaches the end of the climb, doing, perhaps, 35 m.p.h. with its load of about 350 tons.

Just before the train plunges into Blea Moor Tunnel, we notice on the right of the line a cluster of houses—here, without even an approach road, there lives a small railway community, often isolated for days as the storms sweep across these inhospitable moors.

And so, into the darkness of the tunnel, bored under the shoulder of Whernside, the third of the three Ribblesdale Peaks which many a keen walker has done between sunrise and sunset.

Out into the daylight—and what a surprise. This is another world. Gone is the craggy bleakness, no longer the sound of hard labour from the engine. We are over the top and now most of it is on the level until we start the descent from Ais Gill. But, look, away to the west, there stretches a beautiful, kindly, green valley. A kind of Shangri-la. This is Dentdale, and so different from Ribblesdale that it is difficult to realise that you are in the same county.

The train streaks along a kind of terrace at the eastern end of the valley. Dent Station flashes by, over four miles from the village from which it takes its name. Rise Hill tunnel, then we are out over the Garsdale troughs, the highest in England.

All round us the Pennines. We really are riding the backbone of England.

Garsdale Station, the Moorcock Inn, Mallerstang Common, Wild Boar Fell, out of Yorkshire into Westmorland, through some of the wildest and most lovely country in the north of England.

The hamlet of Ais Gill passed, now the train belts down the hill into the Eden Valley. For me, this valley, like another place bearing the name Eden, is a place of temptation. Temptation to hide away here remote from the ugliness of life in the big towns and cities—away from the pit heads, slag heaps, and chimneys which are the continuing feature of life in the South Yorkshire coal field!

If it is ploughing time, we shall notice the rich red earth which has been furrowed: the buildings in this lovely valley are, for the most part, built of the pink sandstone which is quarried locally.

To the east, the high Pennines. Cross Fell and Dufton Pike undulate on the sky line until, in the north east, the land dips towards the Roman Wall from the Solway to Wallsend on the Tyne. In clear weather you can see the Pennines giving place to the Cheviots. This is a wonderfully blue landscape.

To the west—the Cumberland Hills, prominent amongst which is Blencathra, called Saddleback. This wonderful rugged skyline so often crowned with stupendous cloud effects touched by the setting sun.

And so we rattle down the hill passing places with euphonious names like Cumwhinton, Langwathby, Armathwaite and Lazonby. Past Durran Hill into Carlisle Citadel.

That was some station, that was! If you want to know just what sort of station it was, read the first chapter called "Journeys" in Hamilton Ellis's "Trains We Have Loved" (pp. 22–24). What a parade of engines—the London and North Western, the Midland, the North Eastern, the Glasgow and South Western, the Caledonian, the North British, the Maryport and Carlisle. Railways came and went from Carlisle Citadel, and, in doing so, provided for the enthusiast a pageant of locomotive types, a symphony of sound, and a blending of colours to be experienced nowhere else in the British Isles.

In these latter days of steam, Carlisle, as a Border junction, retains something of magic, even though the variety has gone. Here the Pacifics of Stanier and Gresley have arrived and departed: here in this great station there is to be found a true " Portrait of Steam ".

I have described in some detail this journey from the heart of the industrial West Riding to the bracing air of the Borders, because it is one of the most superb railway lines in Britain; superbly engineered and built at a great cost in human labour and life. And soon it is to be no more.

But this is more than miles many of railway track: more than just a way of getting from Leeds to Carlisle.

It is a combined operation of a great company of people. Permanent way men who have cared for the track; men who have stood vigil in the fog; men who have hacked a way through snow drifts so deep that station buildings have been buried; men who have battled with gale and flood.

Oh yes—and a special word for those lengthmen whose "beat" included Blea Moor Tunnel, a place bad enough on the footplate, but infinitely worse for those who have to maintain the track in an atmosphere of lingering steam with water running down the walls of the tunnel.

Men (and one woman) who have manned the lonely signal boxes on these bleak moors, and who have fought their way through the savage elements to their boxes, and have kept vigil through the long winter nights.

And the firemen who have shifted thousands of tons of coal from tender to firebox in order that their drivers should not go short of steam as they pounded up the hill.

I guess there are many young men who are now serving as "2nd men" on the diesels, who would like to have another go with the shovel, and who would shed a few unwanted pounds in the process.

Let our final credit be to those splendid men upon whom has rested the responsibility of driving these trains, in peace and in war: in fine weather and foul. Men from Holbeck and Corker Hill; from Kingmoor and Hellifield, who have played their part (and, surely, the most difficult part) in linking Edinburgh and Glasgow with the Midlands and the Capital. Black 5's and Jubilees, re-built Scots and Compounds, Britannias and Gresley's A3's; all these have laboured up and over these magnificent hills.

No engine, I would venture to say, looked more right in these untamed surroundings than Stanier's re-built Scots. There was about them a blunt, no-nonsense sturdiness that seemed to say "Well, this is hard—but, don't you worry, I can do it".

And the deep beat of those three cylinders was just the right music for the wide open spaces.

I have often ridden the footplates of the "Scots" from Leeds to Carlisle. Some have been rough: some have been dirty: but they have all been masters of the job.

As long as I live, I shall remember the sound and feel on the footplate as the train leaves Hellifield—how you can almost feel the train hitting the bottom of the bank—the sensation of battle being joined as the cut off is lengthened, the exhaust shoots upward, the fireman changes from "little and often" to "more and often", the roar from the chimney—and away we go, Stainforth, Helwith Bridge, Horton in Ribblesdale, Selside, Ribblehead, on to Blea Moor, through the tunnel, and out into the pastoral peace of Dentdale.

Of all my memories of steam, none will live more vividly for me than this.

With the greatest respect to other routes that I have travelled on the engine: Leeds to London, Leeds to Newcastle, Liverpool to London, Carlisle to London, interesting as they all are, none has the character, or offers the excitement, of the old Midland line from Leeds to Carlisle.

There is just one glorious moment, however, on another route. That is the view from the viaduct as the train approaches Durham from the south: preferably on an autumn morning, as that great cathedral stands silhouetted against the eastern sky, rising out of the smoky mists of the City of Durham. This is the very epitome of the north and a prospect that must always fill the north countryman with pride, and cause the stranger to gasp with surprise. For this is one of the great views of Europe.

So, then, my prologue to this Portrait of Steam is the Portrait of a Line: a line on which the steam engine has done magnificent work.

This area of mountain, moor, pot hole, peat, and running water will be the poorer for the disappearance of the steam engine: this man made machine which has fitted so naturally into this wild landscape, and which has, in some curious way, expressed the spirit of the countryside through which it passes.

Up Caledonian at Crawford. Stanier Pacific No. 46231 *Duchess of Atholl*.

ANGLO - SCOTTISH
EXPRESSES

Down Royal Scot nears the top of the climb to Shap Summit. Stanier Pacific No. 46231 *Duchess of Atholl*.

Down Elizabethan approaches Copenhagen Tunnel. A4 Pacific No. 60022 *Mallard*.

Up Elizabethan emerges from Penmanshiel Tunnel. Gresley A4 Pacific No. 60033 *Seagull*.

Down Flying Scotsman leaves King's Cross.
A1 Pacific No. 60156 *Great Central*.

Down Capitals Limited at King's Cross.   A4
Pacific No. 60009 *Union of South Africa*.

Up Mid-day Scot at Crawford. Pacific No. 46243 *City of Lancaster*.

Up Royal Scot at Carlisle. Stanier Pacific No. 46230 *Duchess of Buccleuch*.

Left: A1 Pacific No. 60156 *Great Central* in the locomotive yard at King's Cross Station.

Right (upper): Pre-war shot of the down Flying Scotsman at Finsbury Park. A4 Pacific No. 4489 *Dominion of Canada.*

Right (lower): Down Flying Scotsman picking up after slowing through York Station. A4 Pacific No. 60026 *Miles Beevor.*

Below: Taking water at Beattock Summit. Pacific No. 46230 *Duchess of Buccleuch* on the up Royal Scot.

Down Caledonian passes Camden Sheds. Pacific No. 46239 *City of Chester*.

Left (upper): Up Elizabethan "waits for the off" in Edinburgh Waverley Station. A4 Pacific No. 60024 *Kingfisher*.

Left (lower): Down Flying Scotsman goes steadily up the Holloway Bank. A4 Pacific No. 60015 *Quicksilver*.

Right: Down Royal Scot at Greenholme, near Tebay. Pacific No. 46233 *Duchess of Sutherland*.

Above: Down Mid-day Scot takes water at Dillicar Troughs. Pacific No. 46231 *Duchess of Atholl*.

Left (upper): Up Elizabethan leaves Edinburgh Waverley. A4 Pacific No. 60004 *William Whitelaw*.

Left (lower): Down Royal Scot passing Kingmoor Sheds, Carlisle. Pacific No. 46231 *Duchess of Atholl*.

Opposite: Stanier 5MT 4-6-0 No. 45129 at Scout Green, on Shap, with a northbound freight.

THE BLACK 5s

Bangor to Chester stopping train at Bethesda Junction. Stanier Class 5MT 4-6-0 No. 5346.

Class 5MT 4-6-0 No. 44788 passes Etterby Box at Kingmoor, Carlisle, with northbound freight.

Perth to Euston train picks up after stopping at Beattock
Station. Class 5MT 4-6-0 No. 45011.

Northbound freight at Gretna. Class 5MT 4-6-0 No.
45016.

A4s BETWEEN
THE TUNNELS

Left (upper): A4 Pacific No. 60028 *Walter K. Whigham* emerges from the Gas Works Tunnel with the down Elizabethan.

Left (lower): A4 Pacific No. 60017 *Silver Fox* at Belle Isle with down Leeds and Bradford express.

Right (upper): A4 Pacific No. 60029 *Woodcock* blasts out of Copenhagen Tunnel with down Newcastle express.

Right (lower): A4 Pacific No. 60033 *Seagull* on the down Elizabethan passes A4 Pacific No. 60014 *Silver Link* on its way to King's Cross to take the Flying Scotsman northwards.

GREAT WESTERN

"Hall" Class 4-6-0 No. 6923 *Croxteth Hall* leaves
Shrewsbury with train from Paddington to Birkenhead.

At Old Oak Common, "King" Class 4-6-0
No. 6028 *King George VI.*

In the locomotive yard at Paddington,
"Castle" Class 4-6-0 No. 5042 *Winchester
Castle.*

In the Ranelagh Road locomotive yard, Castle
Class 4-6-0's No. 4079 *Pendennis Castle*, No.
5025 *Chirk Castle* and 2-6-2T No. 6146.

Left (upper): Birkenhead train leaving Paddington. "King" Class 4-6-0 No. 6007 *King William III*.

Left (lower): 4300 Class 2-6-0 No. 7319 leaves Chester with train from Birkenhead to Paddington.

Above: Locomotive Exchanges of 1948. G.W. King Class 4-6-0 No. 6018 *King Henry VI* at Beeston with morning train from Leeds to King's Cross.

Below: "Castle" Class 4-6-0 No. 5063 *Earl Baldwin* sets out from Paddington with train for Kingswear.

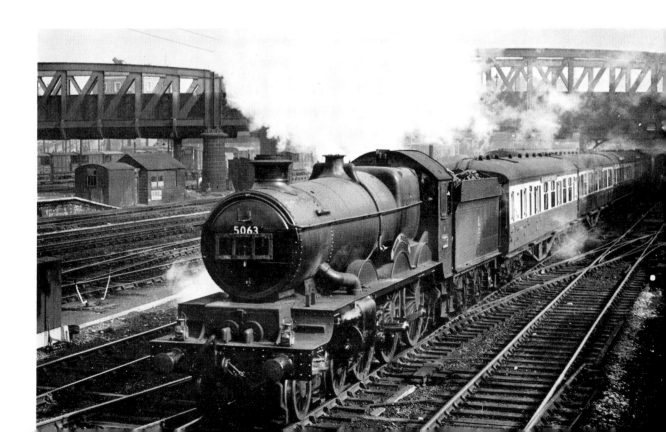

THE ROYAL SCOT 4-6-0s

Above: No. 46146 *The Rifle Brigade* at Holyhead prepared for the up Irish Mail.

Left: No. 46132 *King's Regiment Liverpool* pokes her nose out of the shed at Holyhead.

Below: No. 6103 *Royal Scots Fusilier* at Marley Junction, Keighley, with the down Thames Clyde Express.

Left: No. 46127 *Old Contemptibles* gets a polish at Holyhead.

Below: No. 46125 *3rd Carabinier* leaves Crewe with train from Glasgow to Birmingham.

Left: No. 6170. *British Legion*. Stanier taper boiler re-build of experimental high pressure loco No. 6399 *Fury*.

Above: No. 46146 *The Rifle Brigade* makes a powerful picture as it takes the up Irish Mail out of Holyhead.

No. 46117 *Welsh Guardsman* leaves Carlisle Citadel with the up Thames-Clyde Express.

No. 46112 *Sherwood Forester*. A handsome engine in beautiful condition.

"Preserved". No. 46115 *Scots Guardsman* finds a last resting place at Haworth, Yorkshire, in the care of the Keighley and Worth Valley Railway Preservation Society.

A STATION THAT DIED
LEEDS
CENTRAL

Right: A3 Pacific No. 60039 *Sandwich* at platform 2 with a morning train from Doncaster.

Below: A1 Pacific No. 60119 *Patrick Stirling* sets out with the up Yorkshire Pullman.

Right: A1 Pacific No. 60123 *H. A. Ivatt* makes a run at the Bank up to Holbeck with a train for King's Cross.

Left (upper): A4 Pacific No. 60003 *Andrew K. McCosh* leaves Leeds Central with 9.50 a.m. train to King's Cross.

Left (lower): Leeds to Liverpool train leaves Central. Stanier Class 5MT 4-6-0 No. 45216.

Right: B1 4-6-0 No. 61122 clambers up the hill from Leeds Central to Holbeck with an afternoon train for Doncaster.

Left (upper): Busy mid-day at Leeds Central. A2 Pacific No. 60535 *Hornet's Beauty* sets out for London, as a diesel multiple unit sets course for Castleford.

Left (lower): Down Queen of Scots Pullman reverses in Leeds Central. A1 Pacific No. 60116 *Hal O' the Wynd* sets out for Edinburgh.

Below: An immaculate A1 Pacific No. 60146 *Peregrine* at Platform 5 with a morning train for Doncaster.

Above: A3 Pacific No. 60047 *Donovan* stands by Leeds Central 'A' Box with a mid-day train for London.

Up Elizabethan sets out for London. A4 Pacific No. 60009 *Union of South Africa.*

Up Waverley Express leaves Waverley Station. A3 Pacific No. 60065 *Knight of the Thistle*.

A2 Pacific No. 60536 *Trimbush* emerges from Calton Hill Tunnel with the up Waverley.

Up Flying Scotsman leaves Waverley. A1 Pacific No. 60127 *Wilson Wordsell*.

A3 Pacific No. 60068 *Sir Visto* leaves Edinburgh with train for Carlisle.

Non-stop to London. A4 Pacific No. 60033 *Seagull* sets out with the south bound Elizabethan.

DAYS WITH

NOW IN THE OWNERSHIP OF THE A4 SOCIETY

A grimy Class 5 hauls A4 Pacific No. 4498 *Sir Nigel Gresley* from the shed at Crewe South the day before the Pacific works a special trip from Crewe to Carlisle.

Left: Sir Nigel Gresley moves off from York after stopping to exchange crews on an enthusiasts' trip from King's Cross to Newcastle.

Below: The Pacific stabled between trips at York MPD.

Under the coaling plant at Kingmoor.

On the way north to work a special trip from Glasgow to Aberdeen, *Sir Nigel Gresley* receives attention at Carlisle-Kingmoor.

"On the Table". The Pacific about to be turned in preparation for the return journey.

"Ready for off." The Pacific about to make the return journey to Crewe via Ais Gill, Hellifield and Blackburn.

BEATTOCK BANKERS

Two Class 4MT 2-6-4 tank engines at Beattock Shed.

Class 2P 0-4-4T No. 55187 banking the down Royal Scot at Harthope.

Class 4MT
2-6-4T No.
42215 shoves a
freight train
up the Beat-
tock Bank.

Nearing the
top. Class 4MT
2-6-4T No.
42688 within a
mile of the
summit.

THE DAY THE CASTLES CAME NORTH
—March 4th 1967

The first of the Excursions to arrive at Chester. Castle Class 4-6-0 No. 7029 *Clun Castle* threads the city walls at Chester.

The Second Excursion arrives behind Castle Class 4-6-0 No. 4079 *Pendennis Castle*.

Clun Castle on the triangle at Chester, disposing of stock that did not complete the journey to Birkenhead.

Pendennis Castle, with a full complement on the footplate, disposes of surplus stock at Chester.

At Chester Motive Power Depot. *Pendennis Castle* receives attention: some, expert; some, not!

The two "Castles" at Chester Motive Power Depot.

Pendennis Castle tops up its water tank at Chester.

51

Pendennis Castle moves out of the carriage sidings at Chester before backing into the station and joining up with the train from Birkenhead.

Clun Castle sets out from Chester on the return journey to Paddington.

HOLBECK MPD

"Nose to Nose". Re-built Scot No. 46103 *Royal Scots Fusilier* and Jubilee 4-6-0 No. 45704 *Leviathan*.

Above: Transition from steam to diesel at Holbeck.

Left: Three Class 5's and a Jubilee at Holbeck.

Class 8F 2-8-0 No. 48352 in the Shed.

"Jubilee" 4-6-0 No. 45639 *Raleigh* rumbles on to the turn-table at Holbeck.

Dirty work! The smoke box of a Jubilee 4-6-0 receiving attention at Holbeck.

PORTRAIT OF A FLIER

Mallard moves out of King's Cross Shed for its morning turn on the down "Elizabethan".

Above: The Locomotive Exchanges of 1948. *Mallard* leaves Waterloo with the Atlantic Coast Express.

Below: Morning at Waverley. *Mallard* waits the whistle with the up Elizabethan.

At Portobello East, in the suburbs of Edinburgh, *Mallard* moves south with the up Elizabethan.

NORTHERN FREIGHT

8F Class W.D. 2-8-0 No. 90076 in the cutting at Horbury with east bound freight train.

Above: Britannia class Pacific No. 70015 *Apollo* leaves Wakefield Kirkgate with parcels train for Leed.

Below: Class O2 2-8-0 No. 63985 drifts down the hill between Tingley and Beeston on the outskirts of Leeds.

Right (upper): Class 8F 2-8-0 No. 48119 sets out from York with a freight train for the Midlands.

Right (lower): Class B16 4-6-0 No. 61418 at Dringhouses, York, with southbound freight.

An unidentifiable 8F 2-8-0 at Great Strickland on the West Coast Route.

Class 4F 0-6-0 No. 44469 labouring up Shap with a freight at Scout Green.

Class 3F 0-6-0 No. 57608 leaves Beattock yards with a northbound freight.

B.R. Standard Class 5MT
4-6-0 No. 73102 takes the
G. & S.W. line at Gretna
with freight train.

Between Horbury and
Wakefield, class 4MT
2-6-4T No. 42664.

Class 4F 0-6-0 No. 44079 threads
the city walls at Chester.

Above: Class 7F 0-8-4T No. 7877 leaves Edge Hill goods yards with freight train for Garston.

Below: Class J6 0-6-0 No. 64227 at Grantham

THREE
SUMMITS

Above: SHAP. Pacific No. 46238 *City of Carlisle* with the up Mid-day Scot.

Below: AIS GILL. Re-built Scot No. 46145 *Duke of Wellington's Regiment* with the up Waverley.

BEATTOCK: Class 5 MT 4-6-0 No. 44792 piloting re-built Scot with Glasgow to Manchester and Liverpool train, and (below) Class 5MT 4-6-0 No. 44850 pilots a Jubilee 4-6-0 with train from Manchester to Glasgow.

THE 4-4-0s

Scarborough to Leeds train at Holgate, York. D49/2 Hunt Class
4-4-0 No. 62752 *The Atherstone.*

A pair of Hunt Class 4-4-0's leaving York with a train from Scarborough to Leeds.

Class V Schools 4-4-0

Pickersgill 3P 4-4-0 No. 54503 leaving Edinburgh Princes Street Station with a local train.

Leeds to Morecambe parce
3-cylinder compound 4-4-0 N

Leeds to Harrogate train on the Whitehall curve at Leeds. D49/2 Hunt Class 4-4-0 No. 62773 *The South Durham.*

St Lawrence" at Dover.

Southern Class D 4-4-0 No. 1591 on hop-pickers' special near Hildenborough.

Wortley Junction. Class 4P

TYNESIDE PANORAMA

Up Queen of Scots on the King Edward VII Bridge. AI Pacific No. 60138 *Boswell*.

A1 Pacific No. 60138 *Boswell* at Platform 10 Newcastle Central with Newcastle to Bristol train.

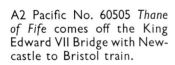

Gateshead MPD. In the foreground A4 Pacific No. 60004 *William Whitelaw*.

A2 Pacific No. 60505 *Thane of Fife* comes off the King Edward VII Bridge with Newcastle to Bristol train.

Newcastle to King's Cross train at Gateshead. A3 Pacific No. 60066 *Merry Hampton*.

Coupling up to the down Flying Scotsman in Newcastle Central Station. A4 Pacific No. 60024 *Kingfisher*.

A4 Pacific No. 60004 *William Whitelaw* heads north from Newcastle with King's Cross to Glasgow train.

A1 Pacific No. 60157 (later named *Great Eastern*) leaves Newcastle with the up Flying Scotsman.

MOGULS

A pair of Gresley's K2 2-6-0's leave Fort William with morning train
for Glasgow. No. 61790 *Loch Lomond* in the lead.

Ivatt 2-6-0 No. 46455 leaves Keswick with train for Penrith and Carlisle.

Class K3/2 2-6-0 No. 61940 at Beeston with Leeds to Doncaster stopping train.

"Crab" 2-6-0 in the Eden Valley at Great Strickland with a northbound freight.

At Banavie with Ben Nevis in the background, K1 Class 2-6-0 No. 62031 with afternoon train to Mallaig.

K2/2 2-6-0 No. 61790 *Loch Lomond* nips along the shores of Loch Linnhe with train from Mallaig to Fort William.

K3/2 2-6-0 No. 61856 leaves Durran Hill yards with freight for Newcastle.

ON THE
FOOTPLATE

Right: An A4 halted at level crossing gates. No. 60034 *Lord Faringdon* at Cromwell, Notts. with up Leeds Express.

Below: Study in concentration. On the footplate of an A1 Pacific heading the up Heart of Midlothian.

Driver Gray of Carlisle Upperby, with whom the author travelled from Euston to Carlisle, prepares Pacific No. 46240 *City of Coventry*.

From the footplate of the North Briton near Neville Hill Leeds. A3 Pacific No. 60036 *Colombo*.

Climbing from Settle to Blea Moor. Rebuilt Scot No. 6108 *Seaforth Highlander* on the down Thames-Clyde.

Pacific No. 46240 *City of Coventry* breasts the summit at Shap with the down Royal Scot.

LIVERPOOL LOOK

Above: Precursor Class 4-4-0 No. 25188 passing Edge Hill MPD with a parcels train.

Left: One of Stanier's 2-6-4 tank engines. No. 42664, drifts down the bank to Lime Street from Edge Hill with empty stock.

Below: Up Merseyside Express passes Edge Hill No. 2 Box Princess Pacific No. 46208 *Princess Helena Victoria*.

Above: All Red and Gold! Streamlined Pacific No. 46235 *City of Birmingham* at Wavertree with West of England train.

Right (upper): Up "Red Rose" leaves Lime Street Station. Stanier Pacific No. 46257 *City of Salford*.

Right (lower): In the cutting. Princess Pacific No. 46204 *Princess Louise* with up Merseyside Express.

Left: The epitome of steam power. Royal Scot engine No. 6143. *The South Staffordshire Regiment*, before rebuilding, at Wavertree with express for Euston.

CROSSING BRIDGES

K3 2-6-0 No. 61985 on the Royal Border Bridge, Berwick-on-Tweed,
with northbound freight.

On the Forth Bridge. A3 Pacific No. 60097 *Humorist* with train from Dundee to Edinburgh.

On the Batty Moss Viaduct at Ribblehead, the down Thames-Clyde powered by Class 5MT and Jubilee 4-6-0's.

A V2 2-6-2 brings a train across the High Level Bridge into Newcastle Central Station.

NINE ELMS MPD

BRITISH RAILWAYS

Left (upper): Merchant Navy Pacific No. 35027 *Port Line* paired with a B.R. Standard 2-6-4 tank engine.

Above: West Country Pacific No. 34100 *Appledore* replenishes its tank at Nine Elms.

Left (lower): Locomotive Exchanges 1948. A4 Pacific No. 22 *Mallard* has its coal ration carefully weighed out.

Below: Interior view in Nine Elms Shed.

LEEDS TO SKIPTON

Left (upper): Down Thames-Clyde Express leaves Leeds City. Re-built Scot No. 46112 *Sherwood Forester.*

Left (lower): Down Waverley Express passes Wortley Junction Box. Re-built Scot No. 46133 *The Green Howards* piloted by Class 5MT.

Above: Leeds to Morecambe train at Holbeck. Jubilee 4-6-0 No. 45568 *Western Australia.*

Left: Down Thames-Clyde Express on the Whitehall Curve, Leeds. Jubilee 4-6-0 No. 45640 *Frobisher* piloting re-built Scot No. 46103 *Royal Scots Fusilier.*

Leeds to Carnforth train at Apperley Bridge. Class 5MT 4-6-0 No. 44812.

Class 4F 0-6-0 No. 44041 with freight train at Skipton South Junction.

Up Thames-Clyde Express south of Skipton.   Re-built Scot 4-6-0 No. 6108 *Seaforth Highlander*.

Re-built Patriot No. 45530 *Sir Frank Ree* passes Skipton with the up Thames-Clyde Express.

SKIPTON TO CARLISLE

Down Waverley leaving Skipton. Jubilee 4-6-0 No. 45686 *St. Vincent*.

Class 5MT 4-6-0 at Horton in Ribblesdale with north bound freight.

A3 Pacific No. 60069 *Sceptre* at Ribblehead with morning train from Leeds to Glasgow.

Britannia Pacific No. 70054 *Dornoch Firth* approaches Blea Moor with down Thames-Clyde Express.

A3 Pacific No. 60069 *Sceptre* at Blea Moor
with the down Thames-Clyde Express.

Class 4F 0-6-0 No. 44094 on the Dent Head
Viaduct with freight train.

Highest main line station in England. A view of Dent Station looking south.

Re-built Scot No. 46112 *Sherwood Forester* heads a Scottish express in typical Pennine country at Garsdale Station. Line to Hawes and Northallerton branches to the right.

Yes—this has been published before, but it is the author's favourite of a Jubilee. In the shadow of Wild Boar Fell, Jubilee No. 45573 *Newfoundland* nears Ais Gill summit with the up Waverley Express.

Jubilee in the Eden Valley near Armathwaite with train from Glasgow to Sheffield.

PACIFICS AT LEEDS

A3 Pacific No. 60112 *St Simon* at Leeds Central with an afternoon train for London. On the left Class 5MT 4-6-0 No. 44692 with train for Liverpool.

Left (upper): Up White Rose, with appropriate front end decoration, at Beeston. A3 Pacific No. 60107 *Royal Lancer.*

Above: Leeds Central to King's Cross train at Copley Hill. A3 Pacific No. 60050 *Persimmon.*

Left (lower): Train for Doncaster and East Anglia on the climb to Ardsley. A1 Pacific No. 60139 *Sea Eagle.*

Below: Blasting out of Leeds on a speed trial to King's Cross. A3 Pacific No. 60056 *Centenary.*

Train for Glasgow leaves Carlisle Citadel. Stanier Pacific No. 46226 *Duchess of Norfolk.*

Above: Down Thames-Clyde Express at Kingmoor. Re-built Scot No. 46117 *Welsh Guardsman*.

Below: A3 Pacific No. 60089 *Felstead* leaves Carlisle Citadel with a stopping train for Edinburgh via the Waverley Route.

Left: Down Royal Scot sets out from Carlisle behind 46231 *Duchess of Atholl*.

Right: Class 3F 0-6-0 T No. 47515 on station pilot duty at Carlisle.

Left: A2/3 Pacific No. 60519 *Honeyway* at Carlisle with a Waverley route train to Edinburgh.

Right: Passing Carlisle No. 4 Box, Pacific No. 46221. *Queen Elizabeth* with Birmingham to Glasgow train.

SCOTTISH SHEDS

Right (upper): Sad sight! Engines stored at Dumfries before being broken up.

Right (lower): St. Margaret's MPD, Edinburgh.

Two shots at the west end of Haymarket MPD

Left: The down Shamrock leaving Euston. Re-built Scot No. 46153 *The Royal Dragoon*.

Right: At the foot of Camden Bank. Royal Scot engine No. 46141. *The North Staffordshire Regiment* with Manchester train.

Right (lower): Is this permitted in a book on steam? A glimpse of the new Euston with the new motive power.

WEST COAST ROUTE

Stanier Pacific No. 46250 *City of Lichfield* at Euston with evening train for Holyhead.

Two Jubilees and a Patriot at Camden MPD.

Right (upper): Down mid-day Scot at Queen's Park. Royal Scot 4-6-0 No. 6147 *The Northamptonshire Regiment.*

Down Scottish Express at Chalk Farm. Streamlined Pacific No. 6227 *Duchess of Devonshire.*

Right (lower): Fylde Coast Express coming off the Whitmore troughs. Jubilee 4-6-0 No. 5734 *Meteor.*

Above: Stanier Pacific No. 46255 *City of Hereford* leaves Crewe with train for Shrewsbury.

Left (upper): Down Red Rose halted at the Crewe approaches. Re-built Patriot No. 45521 *Rhyl*.

Right: Clan Pacific No. 72001 *Clan Cameron* halts at Greskine Box. The reason? Derailment at Beattock Summit.

Left (lower): Liverpool to Euston train leaves Crewe. Re-built Scot No. 46124 *London Scottish*.

Below: Down Coronation Scot at Hartford. Streamlined Pacific No. 6222 *Queen Mary*.

Halting for rear-end assistance at Oxenholme,
Jubilee 4-6-0 No. 45604 *Ceylon* with train from
Manchester to Glasgow.

Class 5MT 4-6-0 No. 45148 on Dillicar troughs with
parcels train.

Southbound freight leaving Preston. Jubilee 4-6-0 No. 45643 *Rodney*.

Class 7F Bowen Cooke 0-8-0 No. 49228 at Lancaster with freight train.

Right: Jubilee 4-6-0 No. 45717 *Dauntless* speeds through Tebay station with Glasgow to Manchester train.

Birmingham Scotsman near Yanwath. Stanier Pacific No. 46241 *City of Edinburgh.*

Re-built Scot No. 46156 *The South Wales Borderer* climbs Shap with Birmingham to Glasgow train.

My best on Shap—therefore it must be included! Wartime shot of down Royal Scot at Shap Wells. Pacific No. 6230 *Duchess of Buccleuch.*

Right: Glasgow to Birmingham train at Hackthorpe. Class 2P 4-4-0 No. 40699 pilots re-built Royal Scot No. 46104 *Scottish Borderer.*

Left (upper): Up Coronation Scot slips down the hill from Shap Summit. Streamlined Pacific No. 6220 *Coronation*.

Left (lower): Locomotive Exchanges 1948. Merchant Navy Pacific No. 35017 *Belgian Marine* makes light work of the down Royal Scot.

Above: Glasgow to Manchester and Liverpool train at Shap Summit. Class 5MT 4-6-0 No. 45017 piloting re-built Royal Scot.

Left (upper): Pacific No. 46240 *City of Coventry* nears Shap Summit with the down Royal Scot.

Right (upper): A spot of cleaning at Carlisle, Upperby. Pacific No. 46237 *City of Bristol.*

Left (lower): Up Perth train leaves Carlisle Citadel. Pacific No. 46256 *Sir William Stanier F.R.S.*

Right (lower): In the woods at Strickland. Stanier Pacific No. 46236 *City of Bradford* with the up Royal Scot.

Inside Carlisle No. 5 Signal box. Signalmen Andrew Johnson (left) and John Trobe.

Pacific No. 46244 *King George VI* comes off the down Royal Scot at Carlisle, and Pacific No. 46231 *Duchess of Atholl* waits to take the train forward to Glasgow.

Re-built Scot No. 46155 *The Lancer* about to be replaced by Pacific No. 46230 *Duchess of Buccleuch* at Carlisle on afternoon train to Perth.

I had to include this one, as it so wonderfully expresses the spirit of Beattock. A grey day and a Pacific fighting its way to the top. Princess Pacific No. 46210 *Lady Patricia* at Harthope with the Birmingham Scotsman.

Above: Up Royal Scot at Crawford. Stanier Pacific No. 46221 *Queen Elizabeth*.

Left: Re-built Scot No. 6108 *Seaforth Highlander* sets out from Carlisle with the down Thames-Clyde Express.

Right: Britannia Pacific No. 70052 *Firth of Tay* makes a smart start from Beattock Station with train from Manchester to Glasgow.

Right and left: Kingmoor Motive Power Depot.

Class 5MT 4-6-0 at Greskine with northbound freight.

Jubilee 4-6-0 No. 45616 *Malta G.C.* at Elvanfoot in the Clyde Valley with Edinburgh to Birmingham train.

B.R. Standard Class 5MT No. 73062 near Abington with freight train.

Re-built Scot No. 46107 *Argyll and Sutherland Highlander* leaves Carstairs with Manchester to Glasgow train.

Clan Pacific No. 72002 *Clan Campbell* approaches Carstairs station with train from Glasgow to Manchester.

Law Junction, Class 3F 0-6-0 (McIntosh, Caledonian) No. 57583 in foreground.

EASTERN PACIFICS

Above: A2 Pacific No. 60535 *Hornet's Beauty* at York.

Below: A4 Pacific No. 60012 *Commonwealth of Australia* at Edinburgh.

Left: Unusual view of Pacific No. 4472 *Flying Scotsman* being prepared for special trip at Doncaster.

Above: A2/2 Pacific No. 60501 *Cock o' the North* at Leeds.

Below: A1 Pacific No. 60161 *North British* at Edinburgh Waverley.

PORTRAIT OF THE PATRIOTS

Above: Re-built Patriot No. 45535 *Sir Herbert Walker* in immaculate condition at Crewe.

Below: A Patriot in its original form. No. 45520 *Llandudno* at Leeds City.

Left: Re-built Patriot No. 45521 *Rhyl* in the Lime Street cutting with the up Merseyside Express.

No. 45526 *Morecambe and Heysham* waits its turn of duty at Carlisle Citadel.

No. 5527 *Southport* thunders through Edge Hill with the 11.15 am Liverpool to London train.

A familiar picture, but I must include it. It breathes the atmosphere of a spring day on Shap. Patriot 45542 (un-named) at Greenholme with freight.

No. 45504 *Royal Signals* at Upperby with train from Glasgow to Liverpool.

Above: No. 45515 *Caernarvon* labours up Camden Bank with a train for Blackpool.

Below: Re-built Patriot No. 45535 *Sir Herbert Walker* tackles Beattock unassisted with Birmingham to Glasgow train.

TWO PULLMANS

Left (upper): A1 Pacific No. 60123 *H. A. Ivatt* about to leave Leeds Central with the up Queen of Scots.

Above: A1 Pacific No. 60117 *Bois Roussel* at Leeds Central awaits the arrival of the Pullman from the North.

Left (lower): Down Yorkshire Pullman belts up the bank from King's Cross. A4 Pacific No. 60028 *Walter K. Whigham*.

Below: Up Queen of Scots leaves Edinburgh Waverley. A1 Pacific No. 60161 *North British*.

Down Queen of Scots at Wortley Junction.   A3 Pacific No. 60072 *Sunstar*.

Up Yorkshire Pullman leaves Leeds Central.   A1 Pacific No. 60136, later named *Alcazar*.

Up Yorkshire Pullman passes Copley Hill Sheds.   A1 Pacific No. 60139 *Sea Eagle*.

SOUTHERN DEPARTURES from CARLISLE

Right: Pacific No. 46221 *Queen Elizabeth* as the non-stop up Royal Scot, halts at Carlisle Upperby to exchange crews.

Below: Pacific No. 46241 *City of Edinburgh* moves out of Carlisle with train for Birmingham.

Above: Pacific No. 46238 *City of Carlisle* passes Carlisle No. 5 Box with up Perth train.

Below: Princess Pacific No. 46204 *Princess Louise* at Carlisle Citadel on train from Perth to London.

Above: A3 Pacific No. 60096 *Papyrus* detaches itself from the up Waverley, which it has brought from Edinburgh.

Below: Rebuilt Scot No. 46135 *The East Lancs Regiment* leaves Carlisle with afternoon train from Perth to Euston.

LEEDS CITY

Left: A3 Pacific No. 60072 *Sunstar* takes the afternoon train from Liverpool to Newcastle out of City Station and approaches Holbeck.

Above: Another pair leaves Leeds City. Hunt Class 4-4-0 No. 62749 *The Cottesmore* pilots A3 Pacific No. 60074 *Harvester*.

Below: A3 Pacific No. 60073 *St. Gatien* uncouples from Newcastle to Liverpool train at Leeds City.

Above: Jubilee 4-6-0 leaves Leeds City with train from Bradford to St. Pancras.

Below: Down Thames-Clyde Express leaves Leeds City behind rebuilt Scot No. 46108 *Seaforth Highlander,* and Jubilee No. 45590 *Travancore* waits to take the up express to London.

Above: Jubilee No. 45646 *Napier* leaves Leeds City with a stopping train to Manchester.

Below: Class B12 4-6-0 No. 61432 leaves City Station with an excursion for Newcastle.

PORTRAIT of the PRINCESSES

Above: No. 46212 *Duchess of Kent* at Crewe North shed.

Left: No. 46205 *Princess Victoria* romps up Beattock from the north with Glasgow to Birmingham train.

Right (upper): No. 46210 *Lady Patricia* leaves Beattock with the down sleeper.

Right (lower): No. 46208 *Princess Helena Victoria* passes Camden Sheds with the down Merseyside Express.

Left (upper): No. 46201 *Princess Elizabeth* at Clifton with the up Birmingham Scotsman.

Above: No. 6208 *Princess Helena Victoria* leaves Edge Hill with Liverpool to west of England train.

Left (lower): No. 46206 *Princess Marie Louise* at Thrimby with train for Birmingham from Scotland.

Below: No. 46209 *Princess Beatrice* at Scout Green with the down mid-day Scot.

EAST COAST ROUTE

Study in steam. A4 Pacific No. 60006 *Sir Ralph Wedgwood* at King's Cross with Leeds and Bradford train.

A3 Pacific No. 60055 *Woolwinder* plunges into the Gas Works Tunnel with express for Leeds and Bradford.

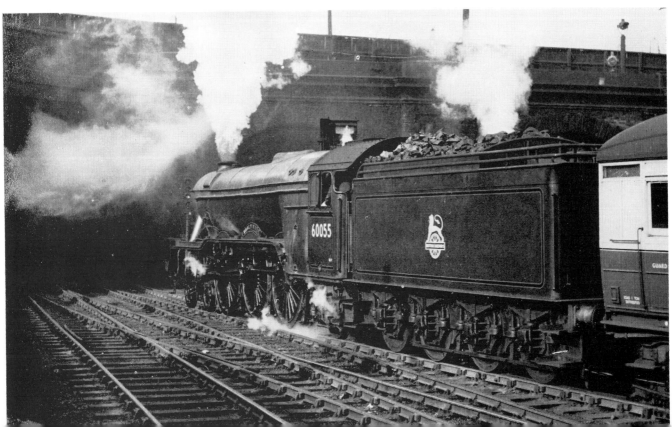

A1 Pacific No. 60128 *Bongrace* leaves King's Cross with evening train for Newcastle.

Morning departure for Newcastle. A4 Pacific No. 60017 *Silver Fox*.

Framed in a signal gantry A4 Pacific No. 60028 *Walter K. Whigham* waits to go down to the station to work the down Elizabethan.

Class W1 4-6-4 No. 10000 approaches Potters Bar with train for Newcastle.

N° 10000

A4 Pacific No. 4901 *Capercaille* (later No. 60005 *Sir Charles Newton*) at Potters Bar with Newcastle train.

Up West Riding slips down the hill to King's Cross. A4 Pacific No. 60026 *Miles Beevor*.

Class O2/2 2-8-0 No. 63946
emerges from Stoke Tunnel
with a coal train.

A4 Pacific No. 60025 *Falcon*
starts from Grantham with a
train from the North East.

A1 Pacific No. 60122 *Curlew*
receives attention at Grantham MPD.

Nice clean start from Grantham, A3 Pacific No. 60053 *Sansovino* moves off with train for Newcastle.

A not very clean Pacific. A4 No. 60013 *Dominion of New Zealand* at Peascliffe with up freight.

A1 Pacific No. 60119 *Patrick Stirling* near Gamston with up Leeds and Bradford train.

Right: Newcastle to London express sets out from York, A3 Pacific No. 60065 *Knight of Thistle*.

A1 Pacific No. 60156 *Great Central* leaves Doncaster with a stopping train to Peterborough.

Class J27 0-6-0 No. 65891 at Holgate, York with freight train.

Right: Seen at York, 2-6-6-2 Beyer Garratt locomotive No. 47968 on a coal train.

Above: Up Heart of Midlothian stops at York. A4 Pacific No. 60005 *Sir Charles Newton*.

Left: In the locomotive yards at York, V2 2-6-2 No. 60954.

Right (upper): V2 2-6-2 No. 60979 leaves York with stopping train to Darlington.

Right (lower): King's Cross to Glasgow train leaves York. A2 Pacific No. 60526 *Sugar Palm*.

Left (lower): A1 Pacific with up Newcastle express: Class 5MT 4-6-0 No. 44776 on York to Bristol train, and J71 0-6-0 No. 68250 on station pilot duties.

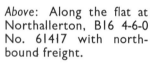

Above: Along the flat at Northallerton, B16 4-6-0 No. 61417 with north-bound freight.

Right (upper): With a train from East Anglia to New-castle. A2/2 Pacific No. 60501 *Cock of the North* leaves York.

Left: A4 Pacific No. 60031 *Golden Plover* on the down Flying Scotsman in Newcastle Central.

Right (lower): Up Eliza-bethan comes off the King Edward VII Bridge at New-castle. A4 Pacific No. 60033 *Seagull*.

Up Capitals Limited passing Tweedmouth. A4 Pacific No. 60009 *Union of South Africa*.

A4 Pacific No. 60031 *Golden Plover* comes off the Royal Border Bridge, Berwick, with the down Flying Scotsman.

And again! A4 Pacific No. 60031 *Golden Plover* on the Cockburnspath Bank with up Flying Scotsman.

Evening train from Leeds to King's Cross at Holbeck. A4 Pacific No. 60032 *Gannet*.

SOUTHERN REGION

Left: West Country Pacific No. 2IC I39 labours up the bank from Victoria to Grosvenor Bridge with Kent Coast train.

Right: West Country Pacific No. 34025 *Rough Tor* at Waterloo with Saturdays only train for Bournemouth.

Below: Lord Nelson Class 4-6-0 No. 859 *Lord Hood* crosses the Grosvenor Bridge with down Boat train.

Above: An immaculate "Lord Nelson" leaves Victoria with a boat train. No. 854 *Howard of Effingham*.

Below: Class N 2-6-0 No. 31855 leaves Tonbridge with train for Charing Cross.

Opposite Page:

Top left: Class H2 Atlantic No. 2424 *Beachy Head* at Hildenborough with train from Hastings to Charing Cross.

Top right: Class E 4-4-0 No. 1491 at Hildenborough with hop pickers' special .

Lower left: Battle of Britain Pacific No. 34082 *615 Squadron* at the coaling stage, Nine Elms MPD.

Lower right: Merchant Navy Pacific No. 35027 *Port Line* at Dover MPD.

Above: Locomotive Exchanges 1948. Merchant Navy Pacific No. 35019 *French Line C.G.T.* with the 7.50 a.m. Leeds to King's Cross train at Beeston Junction.

Below: Bulleid Pacific No. 21C 140 leaves Victoria with the down *Golden Arrow*.

DUCHESSES ON BEATTOCK

Pacific No. 46227 *Duchess of Devonshire* at Longbedholm with the down Royal Scot.

Left (upper): My best on Beattock. Pacific 46250 *City of Lichfield* at Harthope with the down Royal Scot.

Left (lower): With 15 on, Pacific 46227 *Duchess of Devonshire* within 200 yards of Beattock Summit with Glasgow to Euston train.

Above: Early one morning on Beattock. The Euston to Glasgow sleeper greets the morning sun near Greskine. Pacific No. 46223 *Princess Alice.*

EAST COAST TITLED TRAINS

Left (upper): Up White Rose passing the remains of Holbeck High Level station. A4 Pacific No. 60029 *Woodcock*.

Above: Up Talisman leaves Edinburgh Waverley. A4 Pacific No. 60009 *Union of South Africa*.

Left (lower): Up White Rose leaves Wakefield Westgate. A3 Pacific No. 60046 *Diamond Jubilee*.

Below: Up Northumbrian sets out from York. A3 Pacific No. 60092 *Fairway*.

Up Heart of Midlothian leaves Edinburgh Waverley.
A1 Pacific No. 60162 *Saint Johnstoun*.

Up Heart of Midlothian in the woods at Cockburnspath. A1 Pacific No. 60160 *Auld Reekie*.

Down North Briton leaves Newcastle Central. A4
Pacific No. 60002 *Sir Murrough Wilson*.

Up Capitals Limited on the King Edward VII Bridge,
Newcastle. A4 Pacific No. 60003 *Andrew K. McCosh*.

QUINTET OF TANKS

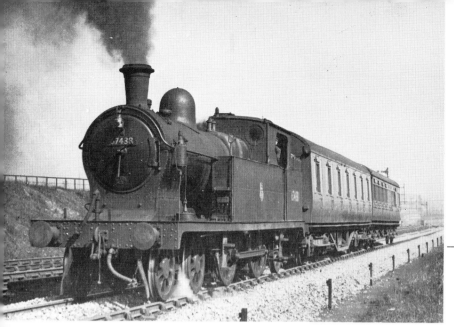

Top: Class C13 4-4-2T No. 67438 (Ex G.C. design) at Copley Hill with train for Castleford.

Left: Class N1 0-6-2T No. 69446 at Copley Hill with train from Leeds to Castleford.

Below: Class N1 0-6-2T No. 69450 leaves Holbeck with train from Leeds Central to Bradford.

Right (upper): Class 4MT 2-6-4T No. 42492 leaves Skipton with stopping train to Carlisle.

Right (lower): Class J50 0-6-0T No. 68900 at Beeston with freight train from Stourton.

Jubilee 4-6-0 No. 45734 *Meteor* leans to the curve as it leaves Penrith
with Glasgow to Manchester train.

Class E4 2-4-0 No. 7416 leaves Penrith with train for Darlington.

Stanier Pacific No. 6232 *Duchess of Montrose* at Penrith with the up mid-day Scot.

Re-built Scot No. 46104 *Scottish Borderer* pulls
away from Penrith with up Perth train.

Stanier Class 5MT 4-6-0 No. 44905 at Yanwath
with southbound freight.

The locomotive yards at York.

A4 Pacific No. 60019 *Bittern* with name plates removed, waits in York Shed for its new owner Mr. Geoffrey Drury.

A1 Pacific No. 60124 *Kenilworth* and Britannia Pacific No. 70012 *John of Gaunt*.

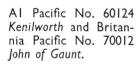

SCOTTISH STATIONS

A3 Pacific No. 60057 *Ormonde* leaves Edinburgh Waverley with train for Aberdeen.

Left (upper): A2 Pacific No. 60536 *Trimbush* leaves Edinburgh Waverley with train for Aberdeen.

Above: Evening scene in Waverley Station.

Left (lower): V3 2-6-2T No. 67624 at Edinburgh Waverley disposing of empty stock.

Above: B.R. Standard Class 5MT No. 73056 leaves Edinburgh Princes Street with stopping train for Carstairs.

Left: Britannia Pacific No. 70054 *Dornoch Firth* leaves Edinburgh Princes Street with train for Carstairs.

Right (upper): A3 Pacific No. 60090 *Grand Parade* at Edinburgh Waverley with the up Queen of Scots Pullman.

Right (lower): A1 Pacific No. 60160 *Auld Reekie* leaves Edinburgh Waverley with the down North Briton.

Class 4MT 2-6-4T No. 80001 (Brighton designed) at Glasgow Central with a local train.

Class 2P 4-4-0 No. 40579 at Glasgow St. Enoch with train for Ardrossan.

STANIER'S JUBILEE 4-6-0s

No. 45565 *Victoria* storms away from Leeds City with the down Waverley Express.

No. 45682 *Trafalgar* at York.

Left: No. 45717 *Daunt-less* leaves Sowerby Bridge station with Liverpool Exchange to Newcastle train.

Right: In the cutting at Milner Royd, near Sowerby Bridge. No. 45717 *Dauntless* with Liverpool to New-castle train.

Front end of No. 45639 *Raleigh* in the sheds at Holbeck.

Left: With northbound freight on Shap No. 45597 *Barbados*.

Right: No. 45726 *Vin-dictive* passes Greskine Box on Beattock with train from Birmingham to Edinburgh.

Above: No. 45670 *Howard of Effingham* passes Edge Hill Station with train for Euston.

Left: Liverpool to Birmingham train at Wavertree. Jubilee No. 5630 *Swaziland*.

Below: Bradford to Bristol train leaves Derby. Jubilee No. 45610 *Gold Coast*.

PORTRAIT OF THE BRITANNIAS

Down Thames-Clyde Express approaches Dent station. Britannia
Pacific No. 70054 *Dornoch Firth*.

No. 70054 *Dornoch Firth* at Holbeck.

No. 70021 *Morning Star* on the ash pits at Holbeck.

No. 70004 *William Shakespeare* leaves Victoria with the
down Golden Arrow.

Under the all-over roof at Wakefield Kirkgate.
No. 70026 *Polar Star* with parcels train.

Left: Study in oil!

Right: Driving wheels of a Britannia at Holbeck.

Below: No. 70015 *Apollo* leaves Wakefield Kirkgate for Leeds with a parcels train.

Below right: Britannia No. 70044 *Earl Haig* at Holbeck Low Level with the down Thames-Clyde Express.

A3 Pacific No. 60079 *Bayardo* pulls out of Carlisle Citadel with the
down Waverley Express.

Class K3/2 2-6-0 No. 61858 near Stow with train of coal empties for the Lothian coal field.

Edinburgh Waverley to Carlisle train at Shankend. A3 Pacific No. 60079 *Bayardo*.

Left (upper): Afternoon train from Edinburgh to Carlisle between Tynehead and Falahill. A3 Pacific No. 60079 *Bayardo*.

Above: Along the Gala Water. BI 4-6-0 with a freight between Galashiels and Falahill Summit.

Left (lower): A grimy A2 Pacific approaches Whitrope with a train from Carlisle. No. 60529 *Pearl Diver*.

Below: V2 2-6-2 No. 60937 sets out for the Waverley Route with a freight train from the Portobello yards.

CLASS EXTINCT
————————FAREWELL, STEAM!